My Cancer

By Angus Olsen

For Jane and Holly

My Cancer

By Angus Olsen

Copyright © Angus Olsen

First published 2020

Published by IDCC

https://idrawchildhoodcancer.com

Written and Illustrated by Angus Olsen

Printed by IngramSpark

ISBN 978-0-6451510-1-5

Weeeeee... oh... hello.

My name is Jane.
Would you like to hear
my story about cancer?

My body, just like yours is made of lots of tiny little things called cells.

Cells help us do everything like running and jumping and breathing and thinking.

One day, when a cell was making a new cell there was a mistake. The new cell was bad.

The bad cell made lots of other bad cells and kept growing, this is cancer.

What can we do about this?

Sometimes we can have special cells made that fight cancer.

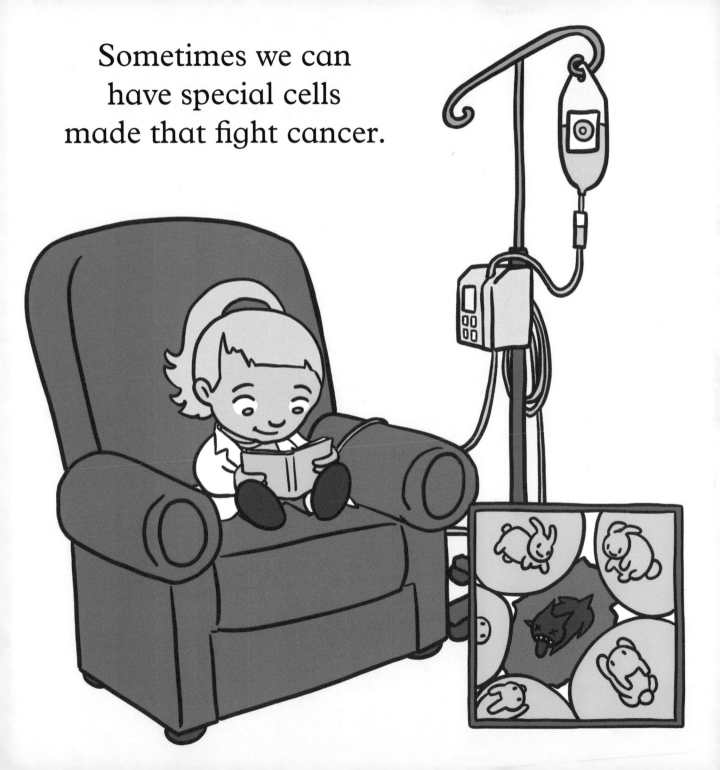

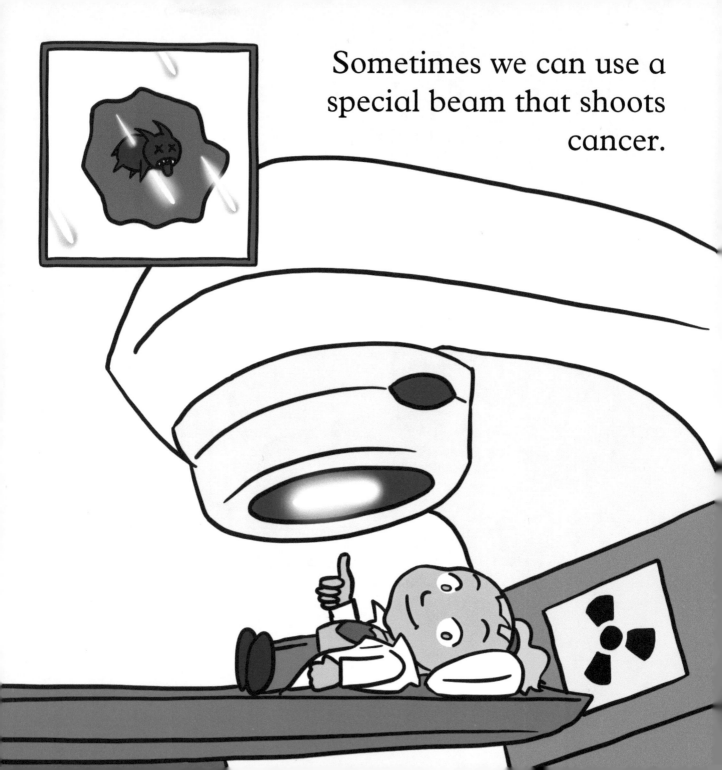

Sometimes a doctor can cut the cancer out. Can you see where my cancer was?

Sometimes we can use
a special medicine
that attacks cancer.

The special medicine
attacks cancer, but it also
makes my hair fall out.

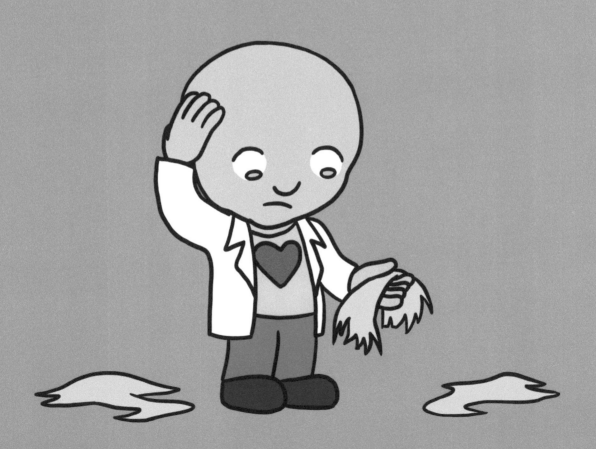

The special medicine also
makes me do lots of vomits.

I have to wash my hands
a lot because I can
get very sick if I don't.

That was my cancer story,
I hope you liked it.

Wait a minute,
why is my head prickly?

Could it be?

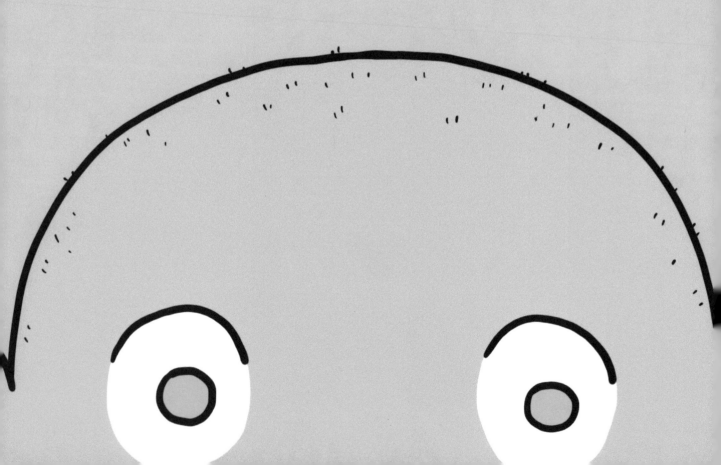

My hair is growing back!

CPSIA information can be obtained
at www.ICGtesting.com
Printed in the USA
BVHW022108060921
615989BV00044B/76

* 9 7 8 0 6 4 5 1 5 1 0 1 5 *